T0195834

MIND FOOD

Retraining Your Thoughts to Win the Battle for Your Mind

GRETA O. KISNER

WestBow Press books may be ordered through booksellers or by contacting:

WestBow Press
A Division of Thomas Nelson & Zondervan
1663 Liberty Drive
Bloomington, IN 47403
www.westbowpress.com
844-714-3454

ISBN: 978-1-6642-6927-9 (sc)
ISBN: 978-1-6642-6928-6 (e)

Library of Congress Control Number: 2022911179

Print information available on the last page.

WestBow Press rev. date: 01/31/2023

WESTBOW
PRESS®
A DIVISION OF THOMAS NELSON
& ZONDERVAN

MIND FOOD

Retraining Your Thoughts to Win the Battle for Your Mind

Foreword

From K-4, "Mommy's Babies"

Our mom prayed to God diligently throughout her life to find her purpose. In addition to being our mother, she wanted to serve the Lord in a mighty way. As her illness progressed and she physically grew weaker, she fought to believe that as long as she was here, God had a use for her. Upon her death, we discovered that she had created and begun publishing this book. It has been a painful journey to finish this work in her absence, but it is a blessing and an honor to complete this in her memory.

This method of taking a negative thought, applying God's Word and holding onto a positive mindset is part of how Mommy helped to instill in us a strong spiritual foundation. That is how this book is intended to be read. Find the detrimental thoughts that resonate with you, read and meditate on the scripture that counteracts it and watch as the power of God's Word transforms your mind and, by extension, your life.

We pray that this book is as much a blessing to you as she was and still is to us.

To Be Avoided

(UNLESS IT'S CONNECTED WITH SOMETHING WRONG)

I CAN'T.

PHILIPPIANS 4:13

THIS ISN'T AS HARD AS IT LOOKS. THE LORD CAN HELP ME FIGURE THIS OUT.

To Be Avoided

GOD WON'T FORGIVE ME.

ACTS 10:43

BECAUSE I BELIEVE IN HIM, I'VE BEEN FORGIVEN. I FORGIVE MYSELF.

To Be Avoided

I HAVE NO CONTROL OVER MY THOUGHTS.

PHILIPPIANS 4:8

I HAVE A BAD HABIT.

ROMANS 6:12-22

I DON'T NEED TO DO THIS. THE LORD'S GOING TO HELP ME CONQUER IT.

To Be Avoided

I'M TIRED OF BEING THE 'BIGGER PERSON.' I WANT TO LOSE SOME WEIGHT.

GALATIANS 6:9

I REFUSE TO MISREPRESENT THE LORD.

To Be Avoided

I HATE HAVING TO (DO SOME CHORE OR JOB).

II Corinthians 9:6

I'M THANKFUL FOR MY ABILITY TO DO WHAT NEEDS TO BE DONE.

To Be Avoided

I'm Broke.

Philippians 4:19

Somehow, God always provides what I need when I need it.

To Be Avoided

I HAVE A BAD MEMORY.

PHILIPPIANS 4:6

THE LORD AND I ARE GOING TO BLOCK THAT THOUGHT FROM ESCAPING.

To Be Avoided

I'M AFRAID.

PSALM 23:4

MY DADDY IS THE BEST PROTECTION POSSIBLE.

To Be Avoided

THEY MAKE ME SO ANGRY.

JAMES 1:20

NO ONE WILL 'MAKE' ME ANGRY. I SHOULD PRAY FOR THEM.

To Be Avoided

I'M STRESSED OUT.

I PETER 5:7

GOD CAN HANDLE THIS. FATHER, PLEASE HELP ME TRUST YOU.

To Be Avoided

I CAN ASK FOR FORGIVENESS LATER.

LUKE 12:20A

'LATER' MIGHT NOT BE AN OPTION. I NEED TO GET IT RIGHT THIS TIME.

To Be Avoided

I HAVE A BAD TEMPER.

EPHESIANS 4:26

IF I CONTROL ANGER, IT WON'T DESTROY ME.

I'M ALONE.

PSALM 139:7-9

WHEREVER I GO, GOD IS WITH ME. I COULDN'T BE ALONE IF I WANTED TO.

To Be Avoided

I HATE FOR PEOPLE TO MAKE ME LATE.

ROMANS 8:28

MAYBE THE LORD IS CAUSING ME TO GET THERE AT THE RIGHT TIME.

To Be Avoided

I'M GOING TO MAKE THEM PAY FOR WHAT THEY DID.

ROMANS 12:19

WHY TAKE ON MORE PROBLEMS? STAY OUT OF GOD'S WAY.

WHY DOES GOD KEEP LETTING THEM GET AWAY WITH DOING WRONG?

ROMANS 2:2-4

I'M THANKFUL THAT GOD IS MERCIFUL TO ME WHEN I'M WRONG.

I DON'T LIKE WHAT I'VE BECOME.

PHILIPPIANS 1:6

I'M STILL THE SAME PERSON. I'LL LET GOD COMPLETE HIS GOOD WORK IN ME.

To Be Avoided

I'M DEPRESSED.

PSALM 34:18

I NEED TO PRACTICE PHILIPPIANS 4:8 AND REMEMBER THAT GOD REALLY IS WITH ME.

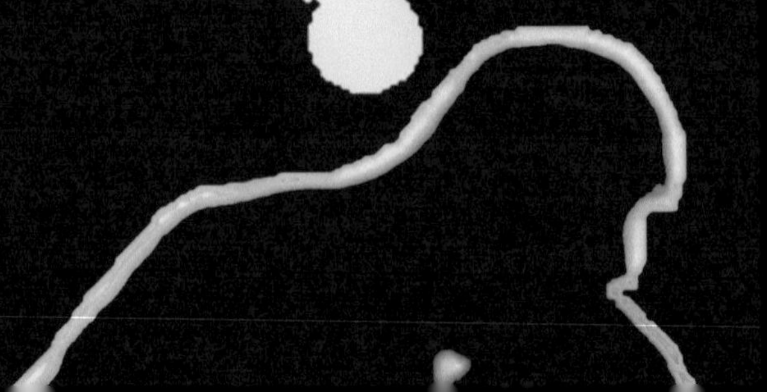

I'LL NEVER FORGIVE THEM.

MATTHEW 6:15

I NEED TO FORGIVE EVERYTHING I'D WANT GOD TO FORGIVE ME FOR.

I'M BETTER THAN THEY ARE. WHEN WILL IT BE MY TURN?

I PETER 5:6

GOD'S PREPARING ME FOR THE NEXT LEVEL AND THE NEXT LEVEL FOR ME.

I'M TIRED OF EVERYONE LYING ABOUT ME.

JAMES 1:19

I'LL ASK GOD TO SHOW ME MYSELF THEN MAKE NECESSARY ADJUSTMENTS.

To Be Avoided

GOD HAS A LOT FOR THE RIGHTEOUS. I'M NOT RIGHTEOUS.

ROMANS 4:23-24

GOD CONSIDERS ME RIGHTEOUS. THOSE PROMISES ARE TO AND FOR ME.

To Be Avoided

I'M GONNA DIE FROM SOMETHING. I'M GOING TO ENJOY MYSELF.

ROMANS 12:1

IF I'M REALLY GOING TO LIVE FOR GOD, I NEED TO TAKE GOOD CARE OF MY BODY TOO.

To Be Avoided

AFTER WHAT I'VE DONE, THERE'S NO WAY ANY ONE COULD LOVE ME.

ROMANS 8:38-39

GOD'S LOVE IS MORE VALUABLE THAN ANYONE'S. GOD AND I LOVE ME.

To Be Avoided

NO ONE HAS ANY IDEA HOW SEVERE THIS TEMPTATION IS.

I CORINTHIANS 10:13

GOD SHOWS US HOW TO ESCAPE. I NEED TO FIND AND FOLLOW HIS WAY OUT.

WHY DOES GOD LET BAD THINGS HAPPEN TO GOOD PEOPLE?

ROMANS 2:11

FATHER, IN SOME WAY, PLEASE DON'T LET THIS BE FRUITLESS.

To Be Avoided

IF ONLY THEY COULD READ MY MIND...

PROVERBS 4:23

EVEN IN MY MIND, I NEED TO CAREFULLY CHOOSE MY WORDS.

I DON'T KNOW HOW TO HANDLE THIS MESS.

PROVERBS 3:5-6

GOD KNOWS EVERY ANGLE
OF THIS. HE'LL SHOW
ME WHAT TO DO.

To Be Avoided

PEOPLE DON'T SEEM TO APPRECIATE WHAT I DO.

COLOSSIANS 3:2

GOD KNOWS MY HEART AND BLESSES ME IN WAYS THAT PEOPLE CAN'T.

To Be Avoided

WHEN I TELL HOW (UNPLEASANT) THEY REALLY ARE...

COLOSSIANS 4:6

FATHER, PLEASE GIVE ME WORDS TO SAY WITH THE PROPER ATTITUDE.

To Be Avoided

I DON'T KNOW HOW MUCH MORE OF THIS I CAN TAKE.

ROMANS 5:3-4

THE LORD MUST BE PREPARING ME FOR SOMETHING HUGE!

To Be Avoided

THEY LOOK WEIRD. I HOPE THEY DON'T TRY TO TALK TO ME.

HEBREWS 13:2

NOT EVERYONE IS AS THEY APPEAR.

To Be Avoided

AS EVIL AS THEY ARE, THEY ALWAYS END UP ON TOP.

ROMANS 9:15

WHAT GOD CHOOSES TO DO IS GOD'S BUSINESS.

To Be Avoided

THEY DON'T SEEM LIKE A CHRISTIAN TO ME.

LUKE 18:9-14

AM I THE TAX COLLECTOR OR THE PHARISEE?

To Be Avoided

I HOPE IT DOESN'T LOOK LIKE I'M DOING SOMETHING WRONG.

I Thessalonians 5:22

To Be Avoided

I DON'T LIKE THE WAY I LOOK.

I SAMUEL 16:7B

GOD'S UNCHANGING PREFERENCES ARE THE ONLY ONES THAT MATTER.

To Be Avoided

THINGS WILL NEVER GET BETTER.

EPHESIANS 3:20

I DON'T KNOW HOW TO MAKE THINGS BETTER BUT GOD DOES AND WILL.

To Be Avoided

I DON'T KNOW IF I SHOULD TRUST THEM.

PROVERBS 3:5-6

THE LORD KNOWS THEM MUCH BETTER THAN I DO. I'LL ASK HIM.

To Be Avoided

I DON'T FEEL NEEDED.

I CORINTHIANS 12

NO ONE ELSE CAN DO WHAT I DO EXACTLY AS I'M NEEDED TO DO IT.

To Be Avoided

WE'RE LIVING FROM PAYCHECK TO PAYCHECK.

MATTHEW 6:31-34

AS WE WORK ON OUR RELATIONSHIP WITH GOD, WE'LL LEARN HOW TO PLAN.

THOSE HYPOCRITES SHOULD BE KICKED OUT OF THE CHURCH.

MATTHEW 7:2-5

I SHOULD SPEND MORE TIME IMPROVING MY OWN SPIRITUAL LIFE.

IF I DID IT IN MY MIND, I MIGHT AS WELL REALLY DO IT.

JAMES 4:17

RATHER THAN FANTASIZE, I'LL WORK TO RESIST SUCH THOUGHTS.

To Be Avoided

IF IT WERE ME, I WOULD/WOULDN'T...

MATTHEW 26:34-35 & 69-75

IF THAT HAPPENED TO ME, I HOPE I'D MAKE THE RIGHT CHOICE.

To Be Avoided

I WANT TO SHOW THEM HOW I FEEL WHEN THEY MISTREAT ME.

EPHESIANS 6:10-18

GOD'S ARMOR WILL HELP ME PRAY FOR THEM AND RESPOND AS I SHOULD.

To Be Avoided

IT DOESN'T TAKE ALL OF THAT TO BE SAVED.

ROMANS 14:1-6

I'LL LEAVE IT TO THE LORD TO TELL THEM WHAT ISN'T NECESSARY.

WHEN WILL OUR HOME BE FREED FROM CHILD OCCUPANCY?

PSALM 127:3

EMBRACING OUR GIFT(S) FROM GOD WILL HELP US CHERISH THESE TIMES.

To Be Avoided

I NEED PEACE.

ISAIAH 26:3

FATHER, PLEASE HELP ME KEEP MY FOCUS ON YOU.

To Be Avoided

THE ENEMY IS GETTING THE BEST OF ME.

JAMES 4:7-8

HE CAN ONLY GET 'THE BEST OF ME' WHEN I LET HIM LINGER.

To Be Avoided

WE'RE NOT GOING TO MAKE IT THROUGH THIS.

PROVERBS 18:21

IF MY WORDS ARE THAT POWERFUL, I NEED TO BE OPTIMISTIC.

Printed in the United States
by Baker & Taylor Publisher Services